Also by Cheryl Miller Thurston

Books:

Homework's Not Another Word for Something Else to Lose
If They're Laughing, They're Not Killing Each Other
Ideas That Really Work!
Surviving Last Period on Fridays and Other Desperate Situtations
When They Think They Have Nothing to Write About . . .

Plays:

The Case of the Colorful Kidnapping
The Fall of Solomon Slime
Mystery of the Suffocated Seventh Grader
Melanie and the Trash Can Troll

Musicals:

A Frog King's Daughter Is Nothing to Sneeze At
Moonlighting Teachers

Hide Your Ex-Lax Under the Wheaties

Cheryl Miller Thurston

illustrated by Joyce Turley

Cottonwood Press, Inc.
Fort Collins, Colorado

Requests for permission should be addressed to:
Cottonwood Press, Inc.
305 West Magnolia, Suite 398
Fort Collins, Colorado 80521

ISBN 1-877673-02-1

Printed in the United States of America

For my mother

Table of Contents

Poems about schools, teachers, kids and education

Hide Your Ex-Lax Under the Wheaties

ide Ex-Lax and beer under Wheaties
and condoms below the Parkay.
Put pregnancy tests and your tampons
under boxes of Budget Gourmet.

Hide hemorrhoid treatments and hair dye
under Cocoa Puffs, cat food or Fritos.
And if you buy douches or Denture Creme,
then slip them below the Doritos.

It's best to be careful when shopping.
It's best to be overly prudent.
Just let down your guard for a second —
and you're bound to run into a student.

She'll shamelessly stare in your basket.
You'll strive to look innocent, cool.
Tomorrow your personal secrets
will be gossip all over your school.

Miss Lee and Mrs. Fuller

iss Lee's rows are straight
    and her cabinets are dusted.
Her blotter is fresh
    and her shades are adjusted.
She always has staples
    and Elmer's and tissues.
She never misplaces
a pass that she issues.

              Mrs. Fuller does.

Miss Lee's books have covers;
    she hasn't lost *any*.
Her book order forms
    come right to the penny.
Her class in assemblies
    is quite in control.
She never miscounts
    or forgets to take roll.

              Mrs. Fuller does.

Miss Lee has a grade book that's neat,
    not a smear.
Her lesson plan book
    is complete for the year.
Her duties for playground
    or lunch never tire her.
She never has principals trying to fire her.

                Mrs. Fuller does.

Miss Lee sees no value
    in things that don't fit.
Her warmest remarks
    run to "Quiet" and "Sit."
She never sparks passion,
    excitement or dreams —
She never sees minds that are
    bursting their seams.

                Mrs. Fuller does.

Row Three, Seat Seven

iss Fox called me Linda.
My name, though, is Claire.
   My underwear's itching.
   My skirt has a tear.

Miss Fox moved me here
to keep Bobby from Boomer.
   My kitten's got ringworm.
   My mom's got a tumor.

I'm absent on Fridays,
but no one asks why.
   My brother got busted.
   I tried not to cry.

LeAnn said I'm weird.
She talked soft, but I heard it.
   My daddy, he beats me.
   I guess I deserve it.

Today Mr. Simpson said,
"How's that girl Claire?"
   Miss Fox said, "Oh, fine.
   I've got no problems *there*!"

I Worry

 worry way too much about
   why so many kids today say "these ones" instead of "these"
   and how that happened and why and when
   and why "these ones" sounds terrible
   but "this one" sounds perfectly okay
And why they say "EKspecially" and "EKcetera."

I worry way too much about
   why "all of a sudden" has become "all of THE sudden"
   and how that happened and why and when
And why so many kids say "supposeBLY."

I worry way too much about why "unh-unh," meaning "no,"
   is now "nunh-uh"
   and how that happened and why and when
And why so many kids talk in questions,
   as in "My report on gorillas?
   I worked really hard on it all weekend?
   And I started to print it out?
   But the computer wasn't, like, interfacing with the printer right?
   And now the paper is stuck in the computer?
   And my dad could, like, FAX it to you from his office?
   If you won't count it late?"

I worry way to much about why "way" has become a modifier,
    as in "way cool" or "way tired" or "way hungry"
And why "hello" is no longer a greeting but a disparaging remark,
    as in
    Question: "Who are the Spice Girls?"
    Answer: "HEL-lo."
And why kids are always "all" something,
    as in "I'm all 'No way,'" or "I'm all 'Get real.'"
And why they don't "say" anymore but instead "go,"
    as in "Then I go, 'Hey, dude!'"
And why "I'm like" has taken such firm hold,
    as in "My dad goes, 'Do you want to go bowling with Mom and me?'
    and I'm like, 'As *if*!'"

I really do worry
    way too much.

Nicknames

he principal's fondly called Hitler.
    The math teacher's Lardbucket Lund.
There's Frog-Face Fellini and Mush Mouth.
    There's Mrs. Attila the Hun.
There's Frankenstein, Faggot and Bozo.
    There's Snaggletoothed Snyder and Bones.
And pretty Miss Just-Out-of-College?
    She's always called Old Lady Jones.

Teacher Down the Hall

e had wonderful ideas about using Shakespeare
to challenge ninth graders,
to inspire them,
to help them understand the human condition
    and appreciate the beauty of the English language.
He had wonderful ideas.
He really did.

He had wonderful ideas about
teaching students to write sparkling prose,
helping them to find their voice
and guiding them —
without the use of any red marks, of course —
in the development of clear communication skills
    and a deep reverence for the power
    of the English language.
He had wonderful ideas.
He really did.

He had wonderful ideas about stating requests in a positive way,
eliminating negatives from his vocabulary,
focusing on the outcomes he wanted,
    rather than on the outcomes he didn't want,
and making students feel that success was always within their grasp.
He had wonderful ideas.
He really did.

But when Brandy, right before class,
    threatened to set Laura's long hair on fire
    if she didn't keep her hands off Adam,
and Melissa, right after class,
    suggested that it wasn't fair for him to count her paper late,
    since she had been skiing in Vail all weekend,
and Josh, during class,
    kept drawing pictures of AK-47s in the margin
    of *Romeo and Juliet*,
and Ryan, during class,
    bragged loudly about how drunk he had been
    over the weekend,
and Dawn, during class,
    suddenly stood up and said,
    "Who needs this shit?"
    and walked out –
He had no idea what to do.
He really didn't.

Day Before Report Card Blues

know I failed the test, Miss Marsh,
But honestly, I read it.
    Who's Huck, you ask?
    Well, gee, let's see –
Could I do extra credit?

Letter Perfect

 lfred, you're reading much better!
Alfred, your workbook's complete!
Alfred, you've learned to write cursive!
Alfred, you've learned to be neat!

Alfred, your grade's sixty-nine now.
Alfred, you're . . . well, I'll be blunt:
Alfred, a seventy's passing.
Alfred, I'm sorry; you flunk.

The Basics

erunds, clauses, interjections,
    participles, verb inflections,
      nouns and . . . What's that, Mr. White?
Yes, it's sad that kids can't write.

Pi, percent and numerator,
    dividend, denominator,
      subtrahend and . . . What's that, Billy?
Balance checkbooks? Don't be silly.

Fugue and rondo, treble clef,
    scale, chromatic, key of F,
      chords and rhythm . . . Question Pat?
Sing? We don't have time for *that*!

Synonyms, syllabication,
    roots and blends, pronunciation,
      speed and phonics . . . What now, Corey?
Well, we *might* soon read a story.

Testing: Stanford, diagnostic,
    comprehensive, hearing, optic,
      verbal, motor . . . Ms. McGuire?
Learning? No, that's not required.

Teacher's Prayer

'm trying to make it to noon, dear Lord,
So give me strength; I can't afford
    to take a bat and bash it in –
    the intercom, I mean – and grin
    and cackle madly as I yell,
    "You interrupting fiend from hell!
Take that and that and that!"

And save me, please, from kids with coughs
    whose parents think they're better off
    in coming, hacking, into class
    and causing all their germs to pass
    from child to child and then to me.
    (I wish that I could somehow be
immune from all disease.)

Assist me, guide me, make me tough,
and let me shrug off stupid stuff –
    like untied sneakers, purple hair
    and kids who holler, "That's no fair!"
    Pep assemblies, knuckle poppers,
    make-up laden teenyboppers,
    homework papers – names omitted,
    kids who say they "baby*sitted*."
    (Yes, there are much worse offenses.
Still, I wish they'd learn their tenses.)

Deliver me from notes
  and from the kids who keep their coats
  on in the dead of spring and fall
  and when it's boiling in the hall –
  And from the whiners and complainers
  and the kids who've lost retainers
  and the question, wearing thin,
of "Do we have to turn this in?"

Forgive me, please, for cheating
  when I said I skipped a meeting
  for some X-rays and some tests.
  (Oh, yes, I know that I transgressed.)
  And for that time I called in sick
  and, Lord, I laid it on so thick
  and sounded weak and nearly dying
  when the truth is I was trying
  for some quick rejuvenating
  time to catch up on my grading –
Please forgive all that, I beg.

And give me, please, a Diet Coke
    at 10:00 A.M. to help me cope
    with eighth grade basic English next,
where not one child can read the text.

And make me patient; keep me sane
    at fire drills held in freezing rain.
    And morning duties, bus and hall –
    I wouldn't miss them much at all
    if you could make them disappear
    and also make it crystal clear
    that no one likes announcements much.
    And maybe, for a final touch,
    you'll help me not to show my rage
when someone asks, again, "What page?"

Attention Deficit Disorder

an *all* my friends' kids really have A.D.D.
    (Unless they are gifted instead)?
Aren't *anyone's* children "rambunctious" or "spoiled"
    (Or "sharp as a tack" or "well-read")?

Expectations

iss Bay sees no evil.
Miss Clay sees no good.
Miss May thinks that everyone's
   misunderstood.

Miss Bay gets the good kids.
Miss Clay gets the bad.
Miss May gets the kids Sigmund Freud
   should have had.

Wishes

I wish I was crabby and cranky like Christy;
I wish I was lazy and loud like Elaine.
I wish I was noisy and nasty like Nathan,
and *then* Mr. Fisher'd remember my name.

Yesterday I Was Just a Presbyterian

esterday I was just a Presbyterian,
a Democrat,
a Triple A Auto Club member,
a loyal Book-of-the-Month Club subscriber.

Today I'm a secular humanist,
   a globalistic-thinking new age liberal,
   a feminazi out to destroy family values,
      subvert our American ideals
      and probably burn the American flag during homeroom
         any day now.

What I did was pass out a book.
What I did was pass out a book about a single-parent family
   with a father who doesn't punish his children adequately,
      who lets his daughter wear boys' clothes,
      who defends a black man against
         the decidedly anti-family charge
            of rape,
   who lets his son hang out with a boy who,
      everybody knows,
         grows up to become a homosexual writer
            in real life.

What I did was pass out *To Kill a Mockingbird.*

Faculty Meeting

nce upon a Wednesday dreary, while I grimaced, weak and weary,
at the papers on my desk and all the trash upon the floor,
while I scowled and sat there snacking, suddenly there came a tapping
as of someone gently rapping, rapping at my classroom door.
"There's a meeting," someone grumbled as she passed my classroom door.
   "There's a meeting. What a bore!"

Ah, distinctly I remember it was in the bleak December
and the smudge of muddy boots had left their mark upon the floor.
Eagerly I wished the morrow; vainly I had sought to borrow
from my chips surcease of sorrow – sorrow for the ninety-four
reports on Poe I had to read and tests I had to score.
   I'd be here forevermore.

So the dismal, daunting, dreary thought of going to a meeting
chilled me – filled me with fantastic terrors often felt before,
so that now, to still the beating of my heart, I stood repeating,
"Maybe this will be a short one; we'll be out of here by four –
we will zip right through our business and be out of here by four.
    I think it happened *once* before."

Presently my soul grew stronger, hesitating then no longer
I arose and walked with purpose to the band room, 604,
where I joined the others sinking into chairs and sadly drinking
cups of weak, insipid coffee as our leader took the floor.
Then he passed out an agenda, cleared his throat and shut the door.
    We were trapped in 604.

Long I sat there, darkness nearing, long I sat there, wondering, fearing,
doubting, doodling, dreaming, thinking, "Pick some milk up at the store."
But the droning was unbroken, and the boredom gave no token,
and the principal, soft-spoken, made me want to teach no more,
as he mumbled indecisively of things he'd said before.
    I tried nicely not to snore.

Then the counselor, so intense, arose and tried to make some sense
of something no one understood and I, for one, would soon ignore.
And I tried to stop my yawning as she carried on and on and
showed us overheads of pie charts and statistics and some scores.
And she asked for any questions, and there were some – twenty-four.
    Hatred filled me, that and more.

So I sat there, ever tenser, dreaming up a super censor,
someone Batman-like, efficient, flying in to take the floor,
who'd say, "Holy Education! Let me give resuscitation!"
And he'd pick me up and fly me out that wretched classroom door,
turning once around and calling out, before our mighty soar:
    "You may torture her no more!"

But at last the thing was ending, with the principal commending
our fine attitudes and efforts. (He was "grateful, to the core.")
When suddenly there shrilled the sound of Miss Leona Hill,
who said before we left she thought we should discuss one item more.
"Our policy on gum," she said, "is one we must explore.
    Let's review it, I implore."

Oh, the argument was heated over what was really needed.
Should we all assign detentions over Dentyne and deplore
the use of Bubblicious gum and all the surreptitious fun
of putting wads of Hubba Bubba under desks and on the floor?
"It's appalling!" said Miss Hill. "We must unite and go to war!
    Aren't there *rules* here anymore?"

Then the faculty divided and the Hill contingent chided
all the "slackers" who decided Hill was "rowing with one oar."
And the argument they uttered, while the Hill contingent muttered,
was that gum was just an irritant they felt they could ignore.
There were other problems, bigger, that the teachers should explore –
    Maybe drugs and gangs, and more.

So the faculty, yet splitting, still is sitting, still is sitting
on the molded plastic chairs inside the band room, 604.
And Miss Hill's eyes have the seeming of a demon's that is dreaming
as she stares at us, still scheming for a way to wage her war.
And I cry out, "That's enough! Now give it up, please, I implore!"
    Quoth Miss Hill then, "Nevermore!"

Except for Last Tuesday

he always plans her lessons to
be clear and thought-provoking, and
she balances each period with
varied things to do.
She's careful to be organized,
to make her lessons lively, and
she schedules time for questions,
for discussions and review.

Except for last Tuesday.

By six o'clock last Monday,
she'd completed all her planning for
tomorrow and she'd written
two new units and a test.
She'd typed another worksheet
and she'd read a stack of essays and
she felt her plans for Tuesday
were among her very best.

Except that she hadn't planned
anything for third period.

She hadn't tackled third hour yet, for
it required some thinking and
she thought she'd plan it later but
for now she'd take a break.
She curled up on the sofa and
she turned on *Law and Order* and,
although she loved the show,
she found she couldn't stay awake.

  Except when the phone rang
  two and a half hours later.

She answered, feeling groggy, and
she chatted with her mother 'til
she suddenly remembered
the banana bread she'd said
that she'd bake for Tuesday's meeting
of the policy committee that
would meet right after school and
got more done when it was fed.

  Except when Al Klippenstein was
  there and wouldn't talk about anything but
  gum chewing and kids with pierced noses.

So she went into the kitchen and
she squashed the black bananas and
she chopped a bag of walnuts and
she soaked a bit of bran.
She measured all the rest and
then she stirred it all together
and she didn't find 'til then that
she just couldn't find her pan.

    Except for last week,
    her sister always returned the things
    she borrowed.

Her neighbors' lights were out and
so she grabbed her purse and drove
down to the market where
she bought a pan, some yogurt and some juice.
She hurried to her kitchen,
put the bread into the oven,
fed the cat and did the dishes,
then came up with an excuse.

    Except that you can't call the truth
    an excuse.

She couldn't plan a lesson.
She was tired and needed rest and
she was sure her brain was weak
and couldn't function one more minute.
She thought, "It's not my habit,
but I'll do it just this once and
I will *not* plan out a lesson;
I will go on in and wing it."

Except that she couldn't resist
coming up with at least a general idea.

She thought she'd use *The Pearl*,
the book her third hour kids were reading
(under protest, for they thought
it rather boring, rather dumb).
Yes, tomorrow she'd relax and
she would lead a class discussion,
for the kids were bound to find
discussing symbolism fun.

Except when she was tired,
she had excellent judgement.

No, in seven years of teaching
she had never been a shirker.
She had never been a teacher who
came in without a plan.
She came to class with goals and
with a map to reach objectives and
she kept her kids on task and
she was clearly in command.

Except for last Tuesday,
when her principal came in to observe her.

Zeke Sat

eke sat,
just sat,
    in eighth grade English for half of one semester
    before he was kicked out of school
        for good.

Zeke sat,
just sat,
    doing no work,
    answering no questions,
    showing no interest in anything at all,
    except,
        briefly,
    Lauren,
        two rows over.

Zeke sat,
just sat,
    though he did win the Halloween costume contest
    with a half-hearted Jolly Green Giant outfit,
        but that was because the girls in the class,
        including Lauren,
    thought he was cute,
        which he was,
    and because the boys were afraid *not* to vote for him.

Zeke sat,
just sat,
    but he didn't hurl obscenities,
    books,
    or the occasional student,
        as he sometimes did in other classes,
    because we had a deal,
    unspoken:
        He would leave me alone, and
        I would leave him alone.

Zeke sat,
just sat,
    but sort of pretended to work by having,
        most of the time,
    a piece of paper on his desk,
    while I sort of pretended to think,
        most of the time,
    that I thought he was doing something
        and didn't look over his shoulder
        or check his work
        or ask him questions, or,
            if once in awhile I did,
        we both understood that it was
            just for effect.

Zeke sat,
just sat,
    and sometimes I would feel guilty
    and break the rules,
    insisting that he actually open a book,
        but he would start to smolder,
        like twigs about to ignite,
    and I would know he was going to explode
    and that there would be no turning back,
        ever,
    if I didn't back off.

Zeke sat,
just sat,
    and I was grateful
    because there were 32 others,
        including one inventive drug abuser,
        two gang wannabees,
        three non-readers,
        a mainstreamed special-ed student who hummed all the time
        and Lauren,
            who wrote notes to Pam about her sexual conquests,
            notes I learned not to confiscate
            because they raised troubling questions
            about the younger generation,
            the future of the world,
            Lauren's health
            and my own knowledge of sex.

My head tells me I should have tried to reach Zeke.
My heart tells me I should have tried to reach Zeke.
    But I let him sit,
    just sit,
        for half of one semester,
        before he disappeared
            forever.

I was probably wrong.
I would probably do it all over again.

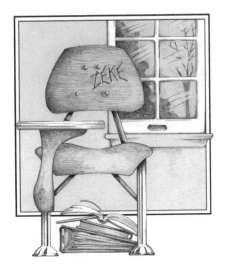

Numbers Game

y twins," complained Millicent Mason.
"They're driving me straight up the wall.
    They make such a mess with their food
    when they're eating.
    They yell and they scream, and
    they're always competing.
    I'm thankful to leave them and
    go to my meeting.
I won't mind an absence at all."

"Good-bye now," said Millicent Mason,
and quickly she let out the clutch.
    She stepped on the gas. As she left,
    she was sighing.
    The twins ran behind. She could hear
    they were crying.
    "I love them," she said, "and
    my love is undying,
but *two* of them's simply too much."

The Board Member Millicent's meeting
was tense; it began with a fight.
    "The teachers," she said, "like to gripe
    and to holler.
    The list of their orders gets
    taller and taller.
    Their classes don't need to be made
    any smaller.
Why, thirty seems just about right."

Some People

have 182 students.
So does Mrs. Kremmling.
But Monday at our staffing on Jake Carmichael,
just as I realized he had never actually turned in the composition
I had been helping him with for two weeks,
Mrs. Kremmling mentioned that three weeks ago last Tuesday
the last paragraph of his homework assignment was a bit shaky,
and she had noticed a decrease in his attention span
on Wednesday mornings
after he returned from his mother's house,
and, oh yes,
the prescription for his glasses probably needed to be changed.

I have 182 students.
So does Mrs. Kremmling.
But last Tuesday at our department meeting,
just as I was thinking about throwing away a stack of papers
because I was so far behind and didn't see how I'd ever get them graded,
and, besides,
the kids would probably never notice anyway,
Mrs. Kremmling mentioned that she had called the parents
of every single student in her classes,
just to tell them something wonderful about their child,
and that three mothers had actually started crying
because no one from school had ever told them
anything good about their children
ever before.

I have 182 students.
So does Mrs. Kremmling.
But Wednesday in the teachers' lounge,
just as I was thinking about
maybe not sponsoring drama club again next semester
because three prima donnas were driving me crazy
and I wanted to start taking an aerobics class in the afternoon,
Mrs. Kremmling announced that she was starting an after-school study group
for kids who needed extra attention
and a little boost toward success,
so if we had any likely candidates for the group
we should let her know,
and oh, by the way,
she had persuaded area merchants to donate snacks for the group,
except on Wednesdays,
when she would bring in homemade brownies herself,
and, oh yes,
she would be taking the group to Denver next week
to see the stage version of *Anne Frank*.

I have 182 students.
So does Mrs. Kremmling.
But last Thursday in my classroom,
just as I was sorting out the third period comma tests
that were mixed up with my seventh period compositions,
Mrs. Kremmling came in and asked
if I had any magenta-colored file folders
because she files the papers of all students
whose last names begin with "D"
in magenta-colored file folders,
and a new student named "Dallabetta" had just registered,
but her order from Office Depot –
paid for with her own money, of course –
hadn't been delivered yet,
and she wouldn't want the new Dallabetta to feel less important
than the other students
because she had run out of magenta-colored folders.

I have 182 students.
So does Mrs. Kremmling.
But Friday in the hallway,
just as I was gagging and trying to get hold of myself
before I summoned the custodian
after Damion threw up,
Mrs. Kremmling,
because it was her free period,
rushed right into my room
and showed the students how to take short, shallow breaths
while we waited for the custodian
and, simultaneously,
erased Damion's embarrassment
and brought his temperature down three degrees
by having him visualize snow-capped mountain peaks.

I have 182 students.
So does Mrs. Kremmling.
But the only person I really can't stand
is Mrs. Kremmling.

Guarding Their Morals

hirty-two people were shot last night
       from seven o'clock to ten.
A psychopath tortured some women,
       then after commercials, some men.

An arsonist burned up a warehouse.
    A hit man erased several thugs.
A porn flick was made starring children.
    A ten-year-old ODed on drugs.

A baby was beaten, in color,
    a teenager raped with a broom.
A businessman's wife was then kidnapped
    and stuffed in a two-by-six tomb.

The kids watch such fare nearly nightly,
    but schools, say the parents, need checks.
"Teach *that* book? My Lord, are you crazy?
    The boy in it thinks about *sex*!"

Awards Assembly

 rack and golf and
    tennis teams.
Swimming, soccer,
    shouts, screams.
Wrestling, hockey,
    trophies, tears.
Baseball, football,
    letters, cheers.

Four-point scholar,
    Ricky White.
Yawns, nods,
    applause, polite.

Conversation in a Shoe Store

e could have just said,
    "May I help you?"
But no – he had to say,
    "Hey, you were my teacher! Mrs. . . . uh . . ."
        And I could have just said,
    "My, but you're all grown up, aren't you!"
But no – I had to say,
    "Hello, uh – now exactly when was it I had you in class?"

He could have said,
    "Oh, a long time ago."
But no – he had to say,
    "I don't remember."
I could have said,
    "It's nice to see you again."
But no – I had to say,
    "Where was it?
    What town?
    What school?"
And he could have said,
    "There's my manager. I'd better get busy."
But no – he had to say,
    "I don't remember."

I could have said,
 "Why don't you show me some high heels?"
But no – I had to say,
 "What subject was it?
  English?
  Social studies?
  Drama?"
And he could have said,
 "We have some lovely new strappy numbers in bright summer colors."
But no – he had to say,
 "I don't remember."

I could have said,
 "How about something in taupe?"
But no – I had to say,
 "What grade were you in?
  Seventh?
  Ninth?
  High school?"
And he could have said,
 "I have just the thing.
  What size do you wear?"
But no – he had to say,
 "I don't remember."

I could have thought to myself,
    "This young man does *not* have a good memory."
But no – I thought,
    "He doesn't remember my name,
        what subject I taught,
        what grade I taught,
        where I taught
        or when.
        I sure made an impression on *him*."
And he could have thought,
    "I may not remember the specifics,
        but did I ever learn a lot from *her*!"
But no – he looked at me like he was thinking,
    "What's the big deal here?
        So what if I don't remember?"

I could have just said,
    "I just remembered I'm supposed to meet someone at Sears."
But no – I said,
    "How about showing me some pumps with a heel,
        in taupe or brown?"
And he could have just taken me to the taupe or brown pumps section
    and turned me loose.
But no – he had to present to me,
    with apparent satisfaction,
    a pair of chocolate suede heels.

I could have said,
> "Thank you. I'll try them on."

But no – I had to say,
> "Sorry, but I really don't like wedge heels."

And he could have said,
> "Let me show you something else then."

But no – he had to say, rather angrily,
> "You used to!
>> You used to wear wedgies every single day!"

I could have thought,
> "He's nuts."

But no – I had to remember,
> "He's right. I had a pair of cork-soled wedgies

that I loved
> in, let's see . . . 1975."

And he could have helped ease an awkward moment with a smile.
But no – he had to look at me as though I'd really let him down.

And I could have helped ease an awkward moment with a smile.
But no – I looked at him resentfully, thinking,
 "My total effect on this young man's life:
  He remembers my favorite pair of shoes from 1975."

He could have remembered *something* I taught him,
 whenever and wherever it was that I taught him.
But no –
 he didn't.

Image

ommy acts tough.
See him strut down his row.
Tommy can't read.
He hopes no one will know.

Peter pretends.
See him puzzle and pout.
Peter's a brain.
He hopes no one finds out.

Jealousy

 arcia's got an office job
and I am plainly jealous.
For Marcia's got a secretary –
Miss Patricia Ellis.

Marcia's got a meeting
to prepare for once a week.
But Marcia's got some help to keep
performance at a peak.

Marcia has reports to do
and she does all the writing.
Marcia writes a draft and then
Miss Ellis does the typing.

Marcia has to supervise;
she's now in charge of four.
Marcia notes their progress
but Miss Ellis notes much more.

Miss Ellis does their records,
every digit and detail.
Miss Ellis types their memos and
Miss Ellis routes their mail.

Miss Ellis also edits and
Miss Ellis sticks on labels.
Miss Ellis runs the Xerox and
Miss Ellis tacks and staples.

Yes, Marcia's got an office job
and I am plainly jealous.
For I have got a teaching job –
but I have no Miss Ellis.

I plan for all my meetings
(There are six of them a day),
deciding what to cover,
what to do and what to say.

I write out all my lessons
and I also do my typing.
I run off all my copies
and I handle my own griping.

I manage and I supervise
a hundred-eighty-four.
I keep up daily records on
each one of them, plus more.

I've got to order staples,
also books and pens and tissues.
I've got to keep abreast of all
the rules the office issues.

I've got to figure grades myself
and screen my mail alone.
And as for making phone calls –
Well, what teacher gets a phone?

Now Marcia's got Miss Ellis
but as any fool can see,
the one who needs Miss Ellis most
is obviously *me*.

Have You Had Your Break Today?

f she had to meet me for lunch on a Saturday
to tell me something important,
I wish it hadn't been that
    she was pregnant by another twelve-year-old
        and afraid to tell her father,
            who would probably beat her up
            again.

If she had to meet me for lunch on a Saturday
to tell me she was pregnant,
I wish I had known how to protect her,
    where to send her,
    how to make everything somehow
    okay.

And if she had to meet me for lunch on a Saturday
to tell me she was pregnant,
I wish that she hadn't been eating a Happy Meal,
    carefully saving the Little Mermaid action figure
    in her paper napkin.

Passing the Buck

here was a professor named Thor
whose ranting was hard to ignore.
    "These kids need essentials
    to reach their potentials,
and that's what the high schools are for!"

A teacher at Hamilton High
saw his students and said with a sigh:
    "They're not over-eager.
    Their knowledge is meager.
Their teachers before didn't *try!*"

A junior high teacher named Pape
taught an hour, then wished to escape.
    "Just look who I've gotten!
    Their test scores are rotten!
These kids are in *terrible* shape!"

The wails from the primary wing
had a sorrowful, pitiful ring:
    "There's something amiss
     when their grades are like this.
The preschools must not teach a *thing*!"

A teacher of tots three and four
shook her head as they shrieked in the door.
    "I find it quite irking
     that parents are shirking
their duties. They ought to do *more*!"

Fluffy White Kitty

 is poems dealt with torture
and with death by bomb or ax.
He loved to make them gory, and
his emphasis was cats.

No matter what assignment
I would give to get him writing,
he wrote about a cat and always
ended with it dying.

He did it with a grin because
he loved to see me groan.
Because I fancied cats,
he wouldn't leave the things alone.

He wrote with wild abandon and
was endlessly quite clever.
But finally I said firmly,
"You can't torture cats forever.

"I want you to expand and
to attempt a new direction.
The subject for today, therefore,
is one of my selection –

"A white and fluffy kitty,
but you can't make this one cry.
You can't let this cat suffer,
and you can't let this cat die.

"With such a lovely topic,
I am confident and trusting
that this fluffy kitty poem
will have nothing that's disgusting."

He listened and he nodded;
then he worked until the bell.
"I've got the title now," he grinned –
"It's 'Fluffy White Kitty from Hell'!"

New English Teacher

There was a new teacher named Tilden
whose handling of kids nearly killed 'em.
He knew conjugations
and long explications
but didn't know beans about children.

Confession

know I'm awful.
I know I'm bad.
I gave in to temptation.
I know I shouldn't,
and I deserve
your rightful condemnation.

I woke up Friday,
grouchy, tired.
I woke up feeling glum.
I didn't want
to teach or
even talk to anyone.

I went to school.
I took my chalk.
I wrote upon the board.
The kids arrived.
I lost resolve.
I did what I deplore.

I had them copy
all the notes
I'd written on the board.
I had them copy
pages, maybe three
or even four.

I did it without shame.
I stood there
brazen and defiant.
I did it for
one reason:
It was just to keep them quiet.

I know I'm awful.
I know I'm bad.
I gave in to temptation.
I know I shouldn't,
and I deserve
your rightful condemnation.

Too Much Morning Coffee

 ight-forty-five.
You won't survive.

Unless you make it out of your room, down the main hall, past Mrs. Romero, through the office, into the restroom, and back – all in four minutes.

You watch the clock.
You get in place.
The bell rings out.
You start your race.

You make it to the door, where Julie wants to know
why she got only an *A-* instead of an *A* on her essay,
since she skipped a flute lesson and stayed up until
2:00 A.M. working on it, and she worries, you know,
about her 4.0 average and getting into a good college
and, like, what will happen if . . .

You cut her off,
but nicely, and
you hurry out the door,
where Larry Hensley waits and
you're afraid you know what for.

He wants you to write down, again, all the
assignments he's missing for the quarter,
which is all of them except for the pop quiz
on commas he failed with a 12%, and because
you've written them down for him twice
already this quarter, with no results, you tell
him you won't do it again, despite the fact
that his mother is going to take away his
mini-bike if he doesn't pass something, and
you point out that he could start by bringing
books, paper and a pencil to class every day,
but he says he hates messing with all that stuff.

You sadly sigh.
You say goodbye.

You hurry down the hallway, ignoring the
smell of cigarette smoke coming out of the
boys' restroom, hoping that what you glimpsed
was not really a *Playgirl* centerfold taped inside
Nicole's locker and congratulating yourself for
arriving at the fight in locker bay number four
right *after* Mr. Bissetti has it firmly under control.

Your head bent down,
you charge ahead.
Then something fills
your heart with dread.

It's Anthony, hanging onto your elbow,
wanting to know if you still have the wooden
sword his older brother Cruz left in your room
two years ago last April when he played
Romeo in the seventh period skit, and do you
know if his class will also get to do a skit, and,
if they do, can he please play Romeo?

You tell him "yes."
You grit your teeth
and, grimly, you press on.
When others call your name,
you look ahead
and don't respond.

Until Mrs. Romero, the attendance clerk,
corners you and asks if Veronica Cooley was
in your fifth hour class yesterday because,
although you marked her absent, she was in
school the rest of the day and it wouldn't be
like her to cut class, so you sigh and admit that
she came in late with a pass after you had taken
roll, and Mrs. Romero shakes her head and
reminds you, again, that you need to mark a
second line through the slash on the
attendance card when someone comes in with
an excused tardy, so you say you'll try to do
better and rush on, through the office, and,
with twenty-three seconds to spare, push open
the door marked "Women" and rush in.

Miss Long's already there.
Despair.

Lesson Plan

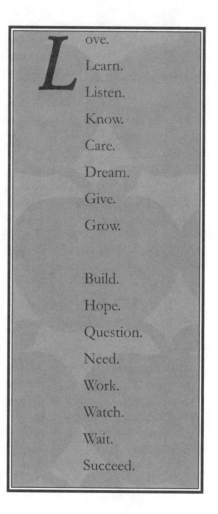

*L*ove.

Learn.

Listen.

Know.

Care.

Dream.

Give.

Grow.

Build.

Hope.

Question.

Need.

Work.

Watch.

Wait.

Succeed.

About the Author

Cheryl Miller Thurston is a former English teacher with over 13 years of experience in the classroom, grades seven through university level. The author of many books for teachers and plays for young people, she lives with her husband and her cat in Fort Collins, Colorado.

To order more copies of
Hide Your Ex-Lax Under the Wheaties

Please send me _____ copy/copies of *Hide Your Ex-Lax Under the Wheaties*. I am enclosing $7.95, plus $3.00 shipping for the first book and $1.00 shipping for each additional book. (Colorado residents add 24¢ sales tax, per book.)

Name _____

Address _____

City _____ State _____ Zip Code _____

Method of Payment:

❏ Check   ❏ VISA/MasterCard/Discover   ❏ Purchase order *(Please attach.)*

Credit card # _____ Expiration date _____

Signature _____

Send to:

Cottonwood Press, Inc.
305 West Magnolia, Suite 398
Fort Collins, Colorado 80521

1-800-864-4297

Call for a free catalog of practical materials
for English and language arts teachers, grades 5-12.

If you enjoyed *Hide Your Ex-Lax Under the Wheaties,* you will enjoy *Music & More by Moonlighting Teachers.*

In 1997, Cheryl Miller Thurston adapted many of the poems in *Hide Your Ex-Lax Under the Wheaties* and included them as part of a full-length musical review called *Moonlighting Teachers.* Made up of a cast of 23 teachers and former teachers from northern Colorado, *Moonlighting Teachers* has been playing to enthusiastic audiences ever since. The group is often invited to perform at local, state and national conferences, banquets and other events.

Now the group has released a CD called *Music & More.* If you enjoyed *Hide Your Ex-Lax Under the Wheaties*, you will enjoy *Music & More*, available through Cottonwood Press, Inc.

Order item #MTCD $15.95

plus $3.00 shipping and handling

To order, call or write:

Cottonwood Press, Inc.
305 West Magnolia, Suite 398
Fort Collins, Colorado 80521
1-800-864-4297